THE CONFUSED QUOTE BOOK

THE CONFUSED QUOTE BOOK

395 Slips, Misses, and Errors Spoken by the High, the Mighty, and Other Celebrities!

Compiled by
GWEN FOSS

Gramercy Books
New York • Avenel

IN MEMORY OF ALAN M. FOSS

This 1997 edition is published by Gramercy Books,
a division of Random House Value Publishing, Inc.,
40 Engelhard Avenue, Avenel, New Jersey 07001.

Gramercy Books and colophon are trademarks of
Random House Value Publishing, Inc.

Random House
New York · Toronto · London · Sydney · Auckland
http://www.randomhouse.com/

Printed and bound in the United States of America

Design by Gwen Foss,
A Push/Pull/Press Book from JSA Publications, Inc.

A CIP catalog record for this book is available from the Library of
Congress.

Foss, Gwen: *The Confused Quote Book*
ISBN 0-517-18502-4

8 7 6 5 4 3 2 1

Acknowledgments

I'd like to thank my parents, Millie Vinitsky Foss and Peter H. Foss, and friends Nancy Kay McHugh and Patricia Dates, who have encouraged and supported me so generously over the years. My romance with irony and error is chiefly due to them. I also acknowledge Mr. Kermit Schafer, renowned collector of broadcasting bloopers, whose book *Bloopers Bloopers Bloopers* was invaluable for ascertaining the correct wording and attributions of several confused quotes that have been handed down through the grapevine. Special thanks to my editor, Susanne Jaffe, and my agent, Joseph S. Ajlouny, for their efforts in making this book possible. And lastly, a big thank you to those whose gaffes are quoted within these pages. Without you this collection would be empty. Touché!

CONTENTS

INTRODUCTION

"I can resist anything except temptation."
Oscar Wilde

The perils fraught in the English language are well documented and debated. Over the centuries they've been discovered, dissected, analyzed, categorized, indexed, and ever-perplexing. This book is a collection of the more ingenious and implausible perils of our ancient, colorful and often maligned language which, after all, is supposed to be utilized to communicate meaning. A professorial linguist might call them "incongruous utterances." A studious composition teacher might call them "irregular usages." A journalistic copy editor might call them "non sequiturs." They have been called, more popularly, "Goldwynisms," in honor of the modern father of the twisted statement, Hollywood mogul Samuel Goldwyn (1882-1974). For present purposes, consider them simply "confused quotes" and be prepared to delight in them.

    Goldwyn was hardly the first person to make an art out of finding the bizarre, oddball meanderings of American English. American-extraodinaire Ben Franklin, an early devotee of words and their meanings, frequently featured clever, funny word pairings such as oxymorons, dangling participles, redundancies, alliterations, and the like in his *Poor Richard's Almanack*. Following in his footsteps was Noah Webster, America's first and greatest lexicographer. While the publication of his *An American Dictionary of the English Language* (1828) is his life's work, he is known to have also collected unusual word usages and phrases that he found defied etymological explanation or classification. "It's a language which never ceases to surprise me," he wrote to his publisher in 1837. "Try as I might to master the beast, I am felled repeatedly, e'er found fleeing to the safety of the vernacular."

    Modern observers of American English words and phrases, including the likes of H.L. Mencken, Charles Earle Funk, John Ciardi, Richard Lederer and William Safire, have popularized the peculiar kinks and quirks to which they are subjected. Countless others, mostly word amateurs, have feasted upon the juicy morsels of ambiguous, distorted, queer or just plain mangled pronouncements that have sprung from mouth and from paper into the heartland. In their wake one suspects they've stirred a special kind of glee, the kind that ignites the spirit of a condemned man after having cheated the hangman. First there's a quiet smile, then a private pause, always followed by a joyful "Hallelujah!" Language does that to people.

The nonsense which comprises this book evokes exactly that kind of feeling. It is humorous, pointed, witty, and usually paradoxical in that it expresses a truth despite the irony of meaning. When Goldwyn said to a pleading director: "An oral contract isn't worth the paper it's written on!" he was being emphatic. His meaning is clear: get it in writing. When Yogi Berra stated, in reply to an invitation for lunch at a new restaurant: "Nobody goes there any more; that place is too crowded," he was politely declining. To a fellow baseball-type, his meaning was probably perfectly understood and its irony undetected. But to the trained ear, both statements (and Goldwyn's more famous "Gentlemen, include me out!") are utterly incomprehensible. They each contain an internal contradiction. Adjectives cross their nouns and adverbs confound their supporting verbs. The result is a mystery of meaning; a mystery, however, which is not all that mysterious. This, then, becomes the defining character of the statements presented here: *A confused quote is the utterance of an undeniable fallacy that nonetheless communicates its intended meaning*.

Other examples are instructive. "Anybody who goes to a psychiatrist ought to have his head examined." Similarly, "I need brain surgery like I need a hole in the head." Both use an inherent truism of the predicate phrase to explain the subjective meaning. "He ate so many apples you'd think they grew on trees" is another illustration of this technique.

Other entries are constructed with a built-in incongruity of possibility. "I had a recurring dream once" sounds plausible. But its meaning is subject to debate and proof. Can one have a recurring dream *once*? Or must it necessarily occur more than once? It's a question as unlikely for resolution as the chicken or the egg debate. "I'd give my right arm to be ambidextrous" is another in this vein. One can, but then one can't, can one?

Yet others contain an irony of purpose. "If my back doesn't get better in a week I'm going to the emergency room" was said by a man suffering pain. "I'll fight him for nothing if the price is right," was how a boxer replied to a reporter's question about his next bout. What they meant is fairly clear. Whether they knew that's what they intended to mean is subject to speculation. But as in every case herein, they said it and that's its beauty.

This collection began many years ago, following a heated family dinner discussion on whether a pie can be *divided in half four ways*. It developed not unlike any collector's passion for her collection, one piece at a time. Before too long a shoe box full of crazy, confused quotes was in hand. A little tinkering, some editing and categorizing followed. The net result is this menagerie of 395 delightful and witty confused quotes.

The first part of the collection focuses on Samuel Goldwyn, the man whose name has been forever linked to the confused quote. His best and most contradictory quotes are presented here, along with short sections on two of

Hollywood's great directors, Michael Curtiz and Gregory Ratoff, who were both noted for their ability to mangle words and their meanings. Part Two contains the confused quotes of baseball star Yogi Berra, who is remembered almost as much for his convoluted elocution as for his athletic prowess.

Part Three, "Puzzling Pronouncements," begins with the confused quotes of the infamous Dan Quayle, former vice president of the United States and first rate Goldwynist, and continues with the oral foibles of many other illustrious stumpsmen and women. It's not surprising that pols are responsible for some of the worst offenses known to the tongue.

The balance of the collection includes confused quotes on a variety of topics. These bodacious gems have been grouped by subject matter and placed into four separate parts, each linked to a general theme suggested by their headings. Though they are bunched together, they are to be enjoyed individually — like delicious grapes — one at a time. As they are digested, the palate cries out for more. Fortunately, this vine is a fertile one. Enjoy!

PART ONE

Goldwyn and his
Hollywood Imitators

Samuel Goldwyn generated a great deal of publicity for himself and his movies by allowing his mastery of mixed metaphors to appear in the press. His verbal blunders were quoted and re-quoted until Goldwyn's publicity people simply began to manufacture them. It is speculated that many, or possibly all, of these loquacious treasures were created merely to generate publicity and Hollywood gossip. Whether these are true Goldwyn quotes or not, they are all exquisite examples of what can happen when one talks faster than one thinks.

Goldwyn speaks!

ON QUITTING:
"Include me out."

ON THE UNOBSERVANT:
"Didn't you hear me keeping still?"

ON SUPERFLUITY:
"Take away the essentials and what have you got?"

TO A FELLOW PRODUCER:
"I ran into your friend last night. He was at my house."

ON SCULPTURE:
"I'm having a bust made of my wife's hands."

ON CONVERSATION:
"Don't talk to me while I'm interrupting you."

ON FRIENDSHIP:
"We'd do anything for each other. We'd even cut each other's throats for each other."

ON SICK LEAVE:
"I've been laid up with the intentional flu."

ON MARDI GRAS:
"Even if they had it in the streets, I wouldn't go."

ON MODERN TECHNOLOGY:
"I'll believe in color television when I see it in black and white."

ON PUBLICITY:
"This will start with a bang in Hollywood and degenerate throughout the whole world."

ON POSTMODERNISM:
"When it comes to ruining a painting, he's an artist."

ON RECYCLING:
"Go ahead and destroy those old files, but make copies of them first."

ON BESTSELLERS:
"This book has too much plot and not enough story."

ON BAD SCRIPTS:
"I read part of it all the way through."

ON BAD ACTORS:
"The scene is dull. Tell him to put more life into his dying."

ON BAD TASTE:
"If Roosevelt were alive, he'd turn over in his grave."

Goldwyn makes a decision.

"I'll give you a definite maybe."

ON PERSPICACITY:
"We'll burn that bridge when we come to it."

ON INSPIRATION:
"I had a monumental idea last night, but I didn't like it."

ON OUTLANDISH SUGGESTIONS:
"In two words: im possible."

Goldwyn negotiates.

ON SOLID DEALS:
"A verbal contract isn't worth the paper it's written on."

ON COLLABORATION:
"I was always an independent, even when I had partners."

TO A NEW COLLABORATOR:
"If you won't give me your word of honor, will you give me your promise?"

ON SALARIED STUDIO EXECUTIVES:
"We're overpaying him, but he's worth it."

ON A PAST DEAL:
"We have all passed a lot of water since then."

ON THOSE WHO DON'T HAVE ULCERS BUT ARE DEFINITELY CARRIERS:
"Anything that man says you've got to take with a dose of salts."

Goldwyn produces.

ON FILM AS ART:
"It's greater than a masterpiece; it's mediocre."

ON ACTION FLICKS:
"I want a movie that starts with an earthquake and works up to a climax."

ON PERIOD PIECES:
"Let's bring it up to date with some snappy nineteenth-century dialogue."

ON LIGHT ENTERTAINMENT:
"Our comedies are not to be laughed at."

ON TALENT:
"Look how I developed Jon Hall. He's a better leading man than Robert Taylor will ever be someday."

ON RUTHLESS MOVIE MAKERS:
"Every director bites the hand that lays the golden egg."

To a screenwriter who revealed the name of his protagonist:
"You're going to call him William? Every Tom, Dick, and Harry is called William!"

To his movie music composer:
"Please write music like Wagner, only louder."

To his writers:
"Let's have some new clichés."

On his Oscar-winning film, 'The Best Years of Our Lives:'
"I don't care if it doesn't make a nickel. I just want every man, woman, and child in America to see it."

Goldwyn talks to the critics.

ON EMPTY PRAISE:
"Tell me, how did you love my picture?"

ON BEING REASSURING:
"I never liked you, and I always will."

TO AN UNDECIDED CRITIC:
"Don't let your opinion sway your judgment."

ON UNEXPLORED TERRAIN:
"I've gone where the hand of man has never set foot."

ON TOTAL AGREEMENT:
"When I want your opinion, I'll give it to you."

ON DISMISSING A CRITIC:
"Don't pay any attention to him; don't even ignore him."

The Confused Quotes
of Film Director Michael Curtiz

Michael Curtiz (1888–1962) directed over 120 films including *Mammy, The Mystery of the Wax Museum, Charge of the Light Brigade, Adventures of Robin Hood,* and *White Christmas.* He was nominated for Academy Awards for *Angels with Dirty Faces* and *Yankee Doodle Dandy,* and he won the Academy Award in 1943 for *Casablanca.* He was born in Hungary and spoke broken English.

INSTRUCTING EXTRAS:
"Separate together in a bunch. Don't stand around so much in little bundles."

DIRECTING AN INTIMATE SCENE:
"Could you get a little closer apart?"

INSTRUCTING GARY COOPER, WHO IS ON A HORSE:
"Now ride off in all directions."

CALLING FOR HORSES WITHOUT RIDERS:
"Bring on the empty horses!"

ON GOOD EXCUSES:
"If I told you the truth, I'd be a hypocrite."

ON STORY CONSTRUCTION:
"You can't do it that way. You spoil the anticlimax."

ON SET DESIGN:
"I want this house overfurnished in perfect taste."

ON A MUSICAL:
"It's dull from beginning to end, but it's loaded with entertainment."

ON HORROR MOVIES:
"When I see the pictures you play in that theater it makes the hair stand on the edge of my seat."

ON HOSTILE CRITICS:
"Everyone wants to jump into my throat!"

The Confused Quotes
of Film Director Gregory Ratoff

Gregory Ratoff (1897–1960) was a Russian-born actor and director who spoke fractured English. He appeared in many films, including *The Corsican Brothers* and *All About Eve*. Among his credits as director are *Song of Russia*, *Moss Rose*, and *Oscar Wilde*.

GIVING A WELL-DESERVED COMPLIMENT:
"You're a parasite for sore eyes."

ON BEING FORTHRIGHT:
"For your information, I'd like to ask you a question."

ON APPEARANCE:
"If she wasn't so skinny she'd be considered thin."

ON CONVERSATION:
"I only talk about the weather in season."

ON THE STRANGE QUALITIES OF SILENCE:
"I want to hear it so quiet we can hear a mouse dropping."

ON SILENCE:
"If you can't keep quiet, shut up!"

"Go see it and see for yourself why you shouldn't see it."

> *Samuel Goldwyn, on a competitor's film*

PART TWO

THE PROPHETIC VOICE OF YOGI BERRA

Second only to Goldwyn himself, baseball star Yogi Berra stands as a testament to the devastating human condition known as *logorrhea malapropia*. If there were a Hall of Fame for utterers of absurdities you can bet Yogi Berra would be a seminal inductee. His confused quotes are popularly known both as *Yogi-isms* and *Berra-isms*.

Yogi Expounds Upon Life

ON CONTINUAL MULTIPLE RE-OCCURRENCES:
"It's like déjà vu all over again."

ON RUNAWAY INFLATION:
"A nickel ain't worth a dime anymore."

ON INCREASING ATTENDANCE AT THE GAMES:
"If people don't want to come out to the ball park, nobody's going to stop them."

ON GOOD INVESTMENTS:
"I bought this large life insurance policy because I'll get it when I die."

ON THE FIRST JEWISH MAYOR OF DUBLIN, IRELAND:
"It could only happen in America."

ON FRENCHMEN IN AMERICAN POLITICS:
"Even Napoleon had his Watergate."

ON UNATTAINABLE PERFECTION:
"If the world were perfect it wouldn't be."

DURING AN ACCEPTANCE SPEECH:
"I want to thank all the people who made this night necessary."

ON SET THEORY:
"Why don't you pair 'em up in threes?"

WHEN ORDERING SWEATERS:
"Gimme one in navy blue and one in navy brown."

ON CLEAR ADMONITION:
"If you can't imitate him, don't copy him."

ON A STEVE MCQUEEN MOVIE:
"He must have made that movie before he died."

ON YANKEE STADIUM IN THE FALL:
"It gets late early out there."

ON PREDICTIONS:
"Predictions are difficult, especially about the future."

ON FOLLOWING DIRECTIONS:
"You've got to be very careful if you don't know where you're going, because you might not get there."

WHEN GIVING DIRECTIONS:
"It's pretty far but it doesn't seem like it."

TO PRESIDENT BUSH AFTER ATTENDING A WHITE HOUSE DINNER:
"How could you get a conversation started in there? Everyone was talking too much."

ON LITTLE LEAGUE BASEBALL:
"It keeps the kids out of the house."

WHEN ASKED WHAT TIME IT WAS:
"You mean right now?"

ON THINGS TO COME:
"There's no stopping the future."

> *On GOLF:*
> "Ninety percent of the putts that fall short of
> the hole don't go in. The other ten percent,
> the wind blows them in."

Yogi Explains the Secrets of His Success

On WINNING:
"The only way to beat them is to outscore them."

On CONCENTRATION:
"Ninety-nine percent of this game is half mental."

On LEARNING:
"You can observe a lot by watching."

ON UNCERTAINTY:
"Uncertainty doesn't bother me as long as we're sure to win."

ON TRAVELING TO A HOME OPENER:
"There's nothing like a home opener, whether it's at home or on the road."

ON PERSISTENCE:
"You give 100% in the first half of the game, and if it isn't enough, in the second half you give what's left."

ON DECISION MAKING:
If you come to a fork in the road, take it.

Yogi Strikes a Defensive Quote

ON HIS OWN SAGGING PERFORMANCE:
"I ain't in no slump, I just ain't hitting."

DEFENDING A FOUL BALL:
"Like hell it was. It was a clean single to the right."

ARGUING WITH AN UMPIRE:
"Anyone who can't tell the difference between a ball hitting wood and a ball hitting concrete must be blind."

ON A BASE-STEALING BALLPLAYER:
"He can run anytime he wants. I'm giving him the red light."

ON A PERFECT GAME:
"It's never happened in a World Series competition, and it still hasn't."

"Our similarities are different."
Dale Berra, baseball player,
comparing himself to his father Yogi

PART THREE

PUZZLING PRONOUNCEMENTS

After dispensing with the confused quotes of the masters we must inevitably turn to the world of politics. While every person in the public eye is capable of committing a Goldwynism, no one has generated so much attention recently as former vice president Dan Quayle. Not all of his widely repeated gaffes qualify as Goldwynisms, but a few of his most confused quotes are lovingly presented here. Then proceeding to England we encounter member of parliament Sir Boyle Roche, whom some have called "The Original Goldwyn" due to the simple fact that he predates Sam by about a hundred years. Finally we reveal America's greatest political misstatements and take a Goldwyn's-eye look at some current issues and the manner in which their discourse has been botched.

The Confused Quotes of Dan Quayle

GREAT OPENING LINES:
"Welcome to President Bush, Mrs. Bush and my fellow astronauts."

ON THE EXPLORATION OF SPACE:
"This is the best planet on earth."

ON BEING PREPARED:
"We are not ready for any unforeseen event that may or may not occur."

ON GEOGRAPHY:
"I love California. I grew up in Phoenix."

ON TRAVELING:
"I haven't been to Michigan since the last time I was there."

ON THE MANY CHAMBERS OF CONGRESS:
"I favor limiting the terms of members of Congress, especially members of the House and members of the Senate."

ON DIRECTION:
"It's a question of whether we're going to go forward to the future, or past to the back."

IN DEFENSE OF HIS TENDENCY TO VERBAL ERROR, MR. QUAYLE SAID:
"I stand by all the misstatements."

Wisdom from Sir Boyle Roche, Britain's Own Goldwyn Mine

ON PETTY DISCRIMINATION:
"If I have any prejudice against the honorable gentleman, it is in his favor."

ON UNFORESEEN DIFFICULTIES:
"The cup of our trouble is running over, but alas, is not yet full."

PROPOSING A NEW LAW TO MAKE TAVERN PATRONS HAPPIER:
"Every pint bottle should contain a quart."

ON THE PROBLEM OF INVISIBLE ASSETS:
"Many thousands of them were destitute of even the goods they possessed."

ON FUTURE ARCHAEOLOGY:
"All along the untrodden paths of the future, I can see the footprints of an unseen hand."

ON MAKING A FIRM PROTEST:
"While I write this letter, I have a pistol in one hand and a sword in the other."

ON IDENTIFYING AND EVISCERATING THE ENEMY:
"I smell a rat, I see him floating in the air, but mark me, I shall nip him in the bud."

ON ANATOMICAL ANOMALIES:
"They intend to cut off our heads and throw them in our faces."

Verbal Massacres from the Political Mind

"Most of our future lies ahead."
> *Harry S Truman*

"I'm not against blacks, and a lot of the good blacks will attest to that."
> *Evan Mecham, former governor of Arizona*

"This is no time to pull the rug out in the middle of the stream."
> *Silvio Conte, U.S. congressman from Massachusetts*

"I was there to make sure all the i's were crossed and the t's were dotted."
> *John Dean, Nixon aide, testifying during the Watergate hearings*

"I can't remember if I told you to stop forgetting."
> *John Mitchell, Nixon aide, on Watergate*

"I have opinions of my own, strong opinions, but I don't always agree with them."
> *George Bush*

"That's why I'll be a great conservative and environmental president. I plan to fish and hunt as much as I can."
George Bush

"I'm not indecisive. Am I indecisive?"
Jim Seibel, mayor of St. Paul, Minnesota

"Democracy used to be a good thing, but now it has got into the wrong hands."
Jesse Helms, U.S. senator from North Carolina

"I'm an armchair naturalist."
James Watt, Secretary of the Interior, Reagan administration

"I don't believe I could have chosen a woman to be vice president who cares more about daycare centers, cares for the deprived and women's rights than Walter Mondale."
Jimmy Carter

"Fluency in English is something that I'm often not accused of."
George Bush

"I want it so that you can't wipe your ass on a piece of paper that hasn't got my picture on it."
Lyndon B. Johnson, demanding blanket publicity

"This strategy represents our policy for all time, until it's changed."
Marlin Fitzwater, former Bush spokesman

"It's time to set aside principle and do what's right."
Dan DeGrow, Michigan state senator, supporting a spending plan

"All day long I do nothing and I still don't get it done."
Ronald Reagan, on retirement

"Sit down and go out."
mayor to a boisterous council member

"If English was good enough for Jesus Christ, it's good enough for me."
U.S. congressman arguing to make English the official language of the United States

"The president of the United States must be an American citizen, unless he was born here."
Leo Rosten, humorist

"Let's get this passed. Later on we can debate it."
George Bush, on a spending plan

"Things are more like they are now than they've ever been."
Gerald Ford

"We are in favor of a law which absolutely prohibits the sale of liquor on Sunday, but we are against its enforcement."
local political platform

"To hell with the public! I'm here to represent the people!"
New Jersey state senator

"That's nobody's goddamned business and you can quote me."
Gen. Harry Vaughan, military aide to President Truman, when asked by reporters about his connections with influence peddlers

"I'm a great fan of baseball. I watch a lot of games on the radio."

>*Gerald Ford*

"When I assumed office four years ago, we stood at the edge of the precipice. Since then, we have taken a giant leap forward."

>*recent president of Brazil, quoted by Jesse Jackson*

"Every man loves his native land, whether he was born there or not."

>*attributed to Thomas Fitch, author*

On Crime

"We need stronger death penalties."
>   *Ross Perot, billionaire*

"Hijackers should be given a rapid trial with due process of law at the airport, then hanged."
>   *Edward Davis, former Los Angeles Chief of Police*

"I wouldn't go downtown alone unless someone went with me."
>   *television newscaster commenting on the high incidence of crime in Seattle*

"A stray bullet killed one bystander slightly."
>   *newspaper story*

"I can't think of any existing law that's in force that wasn't before."
>   *George Bush*

"I'm not guilty and I won't do it again."
>   *Johnny Carson monologue*

"Capital punishment is our society's recognition of the sanctity of human life."
Orrin Hatch, U.S. senator from Utah

"If crime went down 100%, it would still be fifty times higher than it should be."
John Bowman, Washington, D.C. Councilman

"Can you hear me? Squeeze once for yes and twice for no."
police detective questioning severely wounded officer

"Did you get a good look at my face when I took your purse?"
thief who decided to be his own lawyer, questioning the victim during the trial

"Answer this question with a simple yes or no: What were your feelings toward the murdered man?"
lawyer on 'Perry Mason' television series

"Don't go into darkened parking lots unless they are well lighted."
television crime specialist

"When two trains approach each other at a crossing, they shall both come to a full stop, and neither shall start up until the other has gone."
> *railway law*

"We're not the problem — we're just legitimate gangsters."
> *gang youth interviewed on 'Geraldo'*

"The police in Chicago are not here to create disorder, they are here to preserve it."
> *Chicago Mayor Richard Daley, Sr.*

"The more killing and homicides you have, the more havoc it prevents."
> *Chicago Mayor Richard Daley, Jr.*

On Citizens' Rights

"I was afraid the Statue of Liberty would run out."
> *woman explaining her decision to settle a lawsuit*

"The First Amendment guarantees your right to cheat people fair and square."
> *Kurt Thornbladh, attorney*

"I am defending the right of this girl to be judged innocent until she is proved innocent."
> *character on 'Dark Shadows' television series*

"Rotarians, be patriotic! Learn to shoot yourself."
> *journal of the Rotary Club*

"Discrimination is part of American greatness. Inequality, I think, breeds freedom and gives a man opportunity."
> *Lester Maddox, former governor of Georgia*

"I would take my own head by the hair, cut it off, and presenting it to the despot, would say to him, 'Tyrant, behold the act of a free man.'"

anonymous French revolutionary, 1789

On Education

"Say noe to illiteracy."
political slogan

"Tudors needed."

Jim Bacchus, U.S. representative from Florida, in a letter soliciting tutors for high school students

"I took an effective speeching class."
high school student

"Don't use a big word where a diminutive one will suffice."
writing instructor

"Procrastinator's class has been delayed until next Tuesday."

announcement in community college newsletter

"We have homework but we do it in the class."
student interviewed for education survey

On Health Care

"I'm scared to death to get sick."
newspaper headline

"If I died in a hospital, I'd sue!"
Elizabeth A. Johnson, diabetes patient

"The person who is addicted to cocaine responds differently the very first time he uses it."
Dr. David Smith, addiction specialist

"If you think health care is expensive now, wait until you see what it costs when it's free."
P. J. O'Rourke, political humorist

PART FOUR

UNINTELLIGIBLE PASTIMES

Gathered here you will find the world's wisdom applied to the activities of daily life, proof that Sam Goldwyn's spirit still inhabits the homes and workplaces of the nation. Pay careful attention to the manner in which meaning is communicated by default. Perfectly proper statements often require a knowledge of the context in which they were uttered. Mysteriously, these perfectly improper statements don't require such knowledge. They make perfect nonsense under any and all circumstances.

On Literature and Entertainment

"The book is so well written one can hardly understand it."
Lord Byron, poet

"Not a translation — only taken from the French."
Richard Brinsley Sheridan, playwright

"The following poem continues thus…"
Cecile Mermelstein, poet

"It will be noticed that some omissions will also appear in this edition."
Thomas Carlyle, British historian

"Does the album have any songs you like that aren't on it?"
Henry Newt, music reviewer

"Tonight it's Bing Crosby and Carol Burnett together again for the first time."
television announcement

"If you haven't seen it before it's certainly worth seeing again."

> *Millie Vinitsky Foss, legal secretary, trying to talk a friend into seeing one of her favorite movies*

"The show's only a half hour long. You can't do Hitler justice in half an hour."

> *Peter H. Foss, engineer, complaining about the length of a certain television documentary*

"Next Monday night, *Password* will be seen on Thursday evening."

> *Allen Ludden, game show host*

"Wanted: Circus clown with experience. Serious applicants only."

> "I'm an overnight sensation fifteen years in the making."
> *Bob Seger, rock star*

On Haute Cuisine

"I can't eat on an empty stomach."
popular saying

"Just for a change, I'll have the usual."
overheard

"It hasn't been touched by human hands, only me."
Steven Held, broker

> "Food is an essential ingredient to any balanced diet."
> *Terrance Higby, dramatist*

"For this week only, Food Fair is featuring a Passover special on Rath bacon and ham."
broadcast commercial

"I like a french fry with a little meat on it."
Barry Dutter, author

On Faith

"I will now lead you in a few moments of silent prayer."
Bill Peterson, football coach

"God is an atheist."
demonstration poster

"The Garden of Eden is boring as *Hell*."
the Rev. Davidson Loehr

"God, give me patience now."
popular saying

"There will be a procession next Sunday afternoon on the grounds of the monastery; but if it rains in the afternoon, the procession will take place in the morning."
church announcement

"Say *no* to negativity."
> *the Rev. John Corrado*

"I grew up a strict Unitarian."
> *Jennine Lanouette, organizer and activist*

On Sports

"I like football better than baseball. There is less irritation since there are fewer football games."
> *football fan*

"It's surrounded by water on three sides."
> *Roger Twibell, television golf commentator, describing the 16th hole at Hazeltine National*

"Our pitching could be better than I think it will be."
> *Sparky Anderson, baseball manager*

"Today Pittsburgh beat the Pirates, 6 to 6."
> *Vince Sculley, sportscaster*

"I put Sugar Ray Robinson on the canvas where he tripped over my body."

Rocky Graziano, boxer

"Basketball develops individuality, initiative, and leadership. Now get out there and do exactly what I tell you to."

Dick Vitale, coach

"Here comes the pitch — it's a well-hit ball — going straight away center field — going — going — and it's curving foul!"

sports announcer

"I'm the football coach around here and don't you remember it."

Bill Peterson, Florida State coach

"We all get heavier as we get older because there's a lot more information in our heads."

Vlade Divac, basketball player, after putting on weight

"An oversize brassiere might be considered a good investment if you are a runner who breast-feeds a very young baby and became pregnant while running."

U.S. government aerobics manual

"We got reamed inside and out."
athlete on losing a game

"The doctors X-rayed my head and found nothing."
Dizzy Dean, baseball star, after being hit on the head with a ball

"Fans, don't fail to miss tomorrow's game!"
Dizzy Dean

PART FIVE

Unexplainable Perils

Goldwynists don't have more problems than other people, they just sound like they do. The aggravations of time, money and relationships all provide justification for confusion in word and thought. One can't help but wonder if these speakers — and worse, these writers — knew what they were saying when they missaid it.

On Angst

"Is this the party to whom I'm speaking?"
'Ernestine,' portrayed by Lily Tomlin

"I can keep a secret, but the people I tell it to can't."
Anthony Haden-Guest, pundit

"When George Burns said he was a comedian, everyone laughed at him."
Vanna White, television personality

"Solitude's always better with someone else around."
movie character

"Can you be a little more specific in a general way?"
overheard

"I had to sell my saucepan so I could buy something to cook in it."
Woody Guthrie, folk singer

"Let's get out of here and duck!"
>*character on 'Doctor Who' television series*

"Things were run on a need-to-know principle: if you needed to know, you weren't told."
>*Peter Jay, publishing executive*

"I left my beeper at your house. If you find it, page me."
>*Darren Ezzo, restaurant manager*

"Let me know if you don't receive this."
>*George Bernard Shaw, playwright and author, closing a letter*

"There is a lot of information that has to happen."
>*overheard*

"It didn't hurt at first but then I got used to it."
>*Tony Slattery, actor and improvisational performer, 'Whose Line Is It Anyway?' television show*

"I like to reminisce with people I don't know."
>*Stephen Wright, comedian*

"I spent a year in that town one Sunday."
>*Warwick Deeping, author*

"Things are always darkest just before they go pitch black."
character on 'I Spy' television series

"Is this the only original?"
overheard judge

"I'll see that when I believe it."
Deanne Bednar, educator and political activist

"Molenda's last known address was not known."
police report

"I'm a man of very strong indecision."
Oscar Brodney, screenwriter

"Here lies the body of John Mound,
Lost at sea and never found."
gravestone in Winslow, Maine

On Business

"There are no costs, though they have been considerable."
overheard at a business conference

"The tax scheme favors corporations that operate totally or more in North Carolina."
newspaper report

"If the Exchequer persists in taxing the brewing and distilling industries, they will inevitably kill the cow that lays the golden milk."
Sir Frederick Milner, member of British parliament

"If you let that sort of thing go on, your bread and butter will be cut off right from under your feet."
Ernest Bevin, member of British parliament

"He's so greedy, he wouldn't be on an uninhabited island twenty-four hours before he had his hands in the pockets of the naked savages."
British politician

"I'd be happy to discuss the topic further, but I took a vow of silence yesterday."

> *business seminar leader declining to answer questions after his presentation*

On Time

"No one's faster than me. I take my time."
> *Desmond Dorrell Easley, courier*

"As we speak, starting next Monday..."
> *keynote speaker*

"If you want instant coffee, you'll have to wait a minute."
> *Sam Kharsa, furniture salesman*

"Don't do yesterday what you can't do tomorrow."
> *Goldie Hawn, actress*

"How long have you had that birthmark?"
> *Rich Dommers, author and illustrator*

"Her ad lib lines were well rehearsed."
Rod Stewart, song lyric

"She doesn't like me and I don't like her, so it's neutral."
Sean Penn, actor

"The three of us make a great couple."
Ron Wesley, government engineer

"We're married out of wedlock."
Candy Rodriguez, beauty queen

"She couldn't make up a story like that if it wasn't true."
*sister of Paula Jones, who accused Bill
Clinton of sexual harassment*

"I understand that Orthodox Jews don't have sex until
their children are married."
Barry Steiger, humorist

"I'm looking for a meaningful overnight relationship."
Lawrence Nowak, restaurant manager

"If you don't get out of here and leave me alone, I'm going
to find somebody who will."
anonymous fed-up girlfriend

"My wife has a whim of iron."
        Oliver Herford, author

"I'd rather go out with a perfect stranger than go on a blind date."
        Patti Putnicki, humorist

"There's no one more depressed than a happily married man."
        Mickey Rooney, actor

"I've got a man who cheats so much I'm not even sure the baby I'm carrying is his."
        letter to Dear Abby

On Gender Confusion

"You should hear her sing. She's like a female Lena Horne."
Joe Pasternak, film producer

"About half of all babies are boys and girls."
Watertown *(New York)* Daily Times

"Nearly half of our post mistresses are women."
article in a postmaster journal

"You'll never be the man your mother was."
George Burns, comedian

"We're all in this alone."
Lily Tomlin, actress and comedian

PART SIX

INCENSED INVECTIVE

Often the best Goldwynisms are created when we are trying our best to insult, intimidate, or verbally overpower our favorite foes. But beware the boomerang jab — the put-down that can backfire in your face. Here's a generous sampling.

Self-Defensive Confused Quotes

"I couldn't have been drunk; I only had two six-packs."
   motorist pulled over for drunk driving

"Well, if I called the wrong number, why did you answer the phone?"
   James Thurber, humorist

"I can be brainless if I put my mind to it."
   Garnet Rogers, singer-songwriter

"Occasionally I decide to be impulsive."
   Vanity Decklestad, author and folklorist

"I wrote the words; my bass player Slim wrote the lyrics."
   Vincent Beneteau, artist, saxophonist and raconteur, introducing a song

"I'll be right there when I get there."
   waiter, to impatient customers

"Anonymity is my claim to fame."
   Fred Stoller, comedian

"If ever I utter an oath again may my soul be blasted to eternal damnation."
George Bernard Shaw, playwright

"I'm wearing my non-conformist uniform."
Mike Kazaleh, cartoonist

"Profundities are just a guise for people who don't know what they're talking about. And that is profundity."
Cecile Mermelstein, poet

"I know what pot smells like because I've read all about it."
Jessie Munro, author and critic

"No one can shut me up unless they tie my hands behind my back."
Heather Hicks, restaurant manager

"I wouldn't be paranoid if everybody didn't hate me."
Mary Miller, comedian

"Everyone hates me because I'm so popular."
Howard Stern, radio personality

"Necessity is the mother of strange bedfellows."
>*Robert F. Johnson, computer systems operator*

"I don't need an answering machine — I'm never home!"
>*Joseph S. Ajlouny, literary agent*

"Can you keep your voices down so everyone can see?"
>*Bonnie Schorer Clark, auctioneer*

"I'm just talking to myself but no one's listening."
>*Miggy Cohen, small business owner*

"The guy down the street knew I was a pacifist 'cause I had gotten in fights with his son."
>*Walter Jonas, community activist*

"This is a test of the school P.A. system. Will all classrooms that cannot hear me please call the office immediately."
>*Michael Mikula, elementary school principal*

"My whole family's been having nothing but trouble with immigrants ever since they came to this country!"
>*Senator Rawkins, 'Finian's Rainbow'*

"Don't be superstitious — it's bad luck."
>*Finian McLonergan, 'Finian's Rainbow'*

"You'll non-conform when I tell you to non-conform."
film producer

"Last month I blew five thousand dollars on a reincarnation seminar. I figured, hey, you only live once."
Randy Shakes, comedian

"Those aren't commercials, those are advertisements!"
Steve Flynn, Zamboni driver

"I'm gonna be in bed by the time I get home."
Bruce McVey, musician

"Nepotism isn't all that bad as long as you keep it in the family."
Winston Churchill, British prime minister

"My thoughts are going to be no more together now than they will be in a minute."
Lawrence Nowak, restaurant manager

"Cocaine isn't habit forming. I should know, I've been using it for years."
Talullah Bankhead, actress

"He's world famous all over Norway."
> *Theodore Bikel, actor and singer, quoting an*
> *unidentified source*

"There's a certain universality of feeling which is almost worldwide."
> *Marlon Brando, actor*

"As soon as the government starts talking about war, we all get up in arms about it."
> *Johanne Fechter, peace activist*

"Everybody hates me because I'm so universally liked."
> *Peter DeVries, author*

"Don't say 'yes' until I finish talking."
> *Darryl F. Zanuck, producer*

"I didn't break it; I read the destructions!"
> *Stephen Asman, commuter computer tutor*

"He always does improv — he plans it, of course."
> *Whoopi Goldberg, actress and*
> *comedian*

"You know what I hate? Rhetorical questions, that's what I hate."

> *William Jennings Bryan, minister and statesman*

"If God had meant people to go nude they would have been born that way."

> *televangelist*

"It is a folly to expect men to do all they may reasonably be expected to do."

> *Richard Whately, humorist*

"We went to different schools together."

> *William Bryant, department store manager*

"It wasn't important, but it was probably critical."

> *Steven Held, broker*

"Of course I know he's a vampire — I've been trailing him night and day!"

> *movie character*

"I don't want to stir up a hornet's nest with my client as the goat."

> *Milton Clements, insurance adjuster*

"I knew him since before he was born."
L.E. Moir, historian

"Now we're all gonna cooperate and do things my way."
Gerald Edward 'Sarge' Ruppel, U.S. Army

Nasty Confused Quotes

"Did your mother have any children that lived?"
Joan Rivers, talk show host

"How dare you look at me in that tone of voice."
Patti Putnicki, humorist

"I'm not a gossip. That's only a nasty rumor started by the people I talk about."
television character

"If you can't fight nicely then you shouldn't fight at all."
caller to radio talk show

"He's universally loved by dozens."
Utah Phillips, singer-songwriter

"What a show! Every number is better than the
one that follows it!"
Tony Bennett, singer

"Mrs. Long is a selfish, hypocritical woman, and I have no
opinion of her."

Pride and Prejudice *by Jane Austen*

"Hollywood is a great place to call home but I wouldn't
want to live there."
Rod Serling, dramatist

"I'm not self deprecating myself. I might self deprecate *you*,
though."

Reinhold Aman, linguist and lexicographer

"Bless you, Sister. May all your sons be bishops."
*playwright Brendan Behan, on his
deathbed, to a nun*

"I don't believe in astrology, I think horoscopes are crap,
and all of us Libras feel the same way."
astronomy professor

"Must you insist on playing while I'm conducting?"

Sir Adrian Boult, conductor, to a disruptive musician

"You look so natural it must have taken you an hour."
Robert Faris, pundit

"I hate intolerant people."
Gloria Steinum, author

"Please accept my resignation. I don't want to belong to any club that will have me as a member."
Grouch Marx, comedian

"I belong to no organized party. I'm a Democrat."
Will Rogers, humorist

"My psychiatrist said I have a persecution complex. He only said it because he hates me."
Woody Allen, comedian

"Damn your potty mouth!"
Dusty Rumsey, cartoonist

"I loved that meal. Let's never have it again."
Amy Seidel, artist

"You can go with me or we can go together; it's up to you."
Henry Clerval, professor of literature

"I'll have no yelling in here!!"
Kevin Garrison, airline pilot and author

"I'm not trying to belittle you, I just want to knock you down to size."
Ann Teufel, curmudgeon

"Yeah, keep me up when I can't sleep!"
Kathleen Jacobs, student

"I'm always open to honest criticism from you judgmental creeps."
Robert Altman, filmmaker

"Try to use a little tact, you fathead!"
Burt Reynolds, movie star

"It's good to know I can always depend on your half-hearted support."

Ashleigh Brilliant, epigramist

Demanding Confused Quotes

"I wanna see some toleration around here or I'm gonna bust some heads."

overheard

"You call this a script? Give me a couple of $5,000-a-week writers and I'll write it myself."

Joe Pasternak, film producer

"We demand rigidly defined areas of doubt and uncertainty."

Douglas Adams, author

"Just shut up and tell me what he said!"
            Judge Joseph Wapner, 'The People's Court'

"You're gonna enjoy yourself whether you like it
or not."
            Allan Sherman, singer and parodist

PART SEVEN

ARGUMENTATIVE AFFIRMATIONS

Now that we have seen the terrible effects of the boomerang jab we must examine the even more dangerous ricochet wind. The only thing worse than a mangled insult is a misspoken gloat. Witness...

On Modesty

"Modesty is my best quality."
Jack Benny, comedian

"Humility is something I've always prided myself on."
Bernie Kosar, quarterback

"I'll admit I was never wrong."
Cher, singer and actress

"There is only one book on humility. I wrote it myself."
James Ullathorne, former Archbishop of Canterbury

"I love it when I get a surprise gift, especially if it's something I picked out."
Suzanne Somers, actress and talk show host

"One must not be a name-dropper, as Her Majesty remarked to me a luncheon yesterday.
Norman St. John-Stevas, British member of parliament

"I may not always be right, but I'm never wrong."
Isaac Asimov, author and futurist

"The meaning of life is to seek fulfillment of one's personal goals. My personal goal is to discover the meaning of life."
Deborah Bray, student

"If only we could get rid of our arrogance, we'd be perfect!"
Robert H. Nelson, attorney

"This award isn't mine alone — it's just as much for Susan and Margaret, so it's really for all three of me."
anonymous actress

"I thought I was wrong once but I was mistaken."
Lee Iacocca, former Chrysler Corporation C.E.O.

"Consensus is when we have a discussion then I decide."
Lee Iacocca

> "'The more articulate, the less said' is an old
> Chinese proverb which I just made up myself."
> *Don Herald, author*

On Truth

"A true story, based on fiction."
   movie caption

"I had to lie to pass the polygraph test."
   anonymous

"I do not mind lying, but I hate inaccuracy."
   Samuel Butler, author

"Our opinion can be substantiated with a rumor."
   overheard

"The most important thing is to tell the truth, even if you
have to lie to do it."
   Jessie Munro, author and critic

"I don't want to tell you any half-truths unless they're
completely accurate."

Dennis Rappaport, boxing manager

> "I was told that half of the members would be
> eager to get involved, and half of them would be
> apathetic. But after being president for four
> years, I found that just the opposite was true."
> *president of hobby club*

On Death

"And now a record by Glenn Miller, who became a legend in
his own lifetime by his untimely death."

Nicholas Parsons, BBC announcer

"Death is nature's way of telling you to slow down."

bathroom graffito

"He's got rigor mortis? Oh, that's a healthy sign!"

overheard

"All life is sacred and we're willing to kill for it."
anonymous pro-life activist

"The suspect was dead before he knew it."
police dispatch

"He had the same condition I've got, only mine is much worse."
overheard at a funeral

"I can never remember whether it was you or your brother who was killed in the war."
overheard at a family reunion

"People are dying today who have never died before."
member of New York City Council, defending a plan to sell souvenirs of dead celebrities to help fund the city morgue

"If you live to the age of a hundred you have it made, because very few people die past the age of a hundred."
George Burns, comedian

"Once you're dead you're made for life."
Jimi Hendrix, rock star

"If I could drop dead right now, I'd be the happiest man alive!"
> *Pete Townshend, rock star*

"I couldn't live with the thought of killing myself."
> *Peter Sellers, actor*

"If he knew, the current Pope would turn over in his grave."
> *Sylvan Zaft, film producer*

"If you don't go to other people's funerals, they won't come to yours."
> *Clarence Day, author*

"The only way to stop this suicide wave is to make it a capital offense punishable by death."
> *member of the British parliament*

On Math and Statistics

"We'll have to break it down into one piece."
> *overheard*

"Forty-three percent of all statistics are worthless."
> *Dale Kriebel, educator*

"We have only one person to blame, and that's each other."
>   *Barry Beck, hockey player, after a fight on*
>   *the ice*

"If you can tell me how many marbles I have behind my back, I'll give you both of them!"
>   *summer camp counselor*

"There is no exception to the rule that every rule has an exception."
>   *attributed to James Thurber, author*

"The interests of the employers and the employed are the same ninety-nine times out of ten."
>   *Lord Curzon, British member of parliament*

"I've been waiting twenty minutes — you told me you'd be here in an hour!"
>   *real estate agent to his tardy appointment*

"At least half of our customers who fly to New York come by plane."
>   *contestant on Groucho Marx show*

"There's one thing you are: you're hot and you're game."
>   *Angie Dickinson, to herself on arriving in*
>   *Hollywood as an ambitious young actress*

"The bill was forty-one dollars?! You could've halved it by ten bucks!"

Karen Schanerberger, singer

"There are three kinds of people: those who can count and those who can't."

overheard

"Winning is about ninety percent strength and forty percent technique."

Johnny Walker, boxer

Wild Advertising Claims

"We give you service and support 365 days a week."

ad for computer software

"Later is now."

ad for computer store

"Now only $3.95 — this beautiful genuine faux pearl necklace!"

> *jewelry ad*

"If it's in stock we got it."

> *ad slogan of tire supply house*

"This powerful talisman brings money to you, just $6.00 postpaid."

> *ad in New Age catalog*

"We have to reach back into the future."

> *computer salesman at trade show*

"My wife was at death's door and one bottle of your medicine pulled her through."

> *product endorsement*

Confused Messages Meant for Public Edification

"There will be an organizational meeting of anarchists Tuesday evening."

> *announcement in a community college newsletter*

"Members and Non-Members Only"
sign outside Mexican disco

"Members will refrain from picking up lost balls until they
have stopped rolling."
sign at golf course

"Closed due to illness."
*sign at health
food store*

"Women are prohibited from wearing slacks in the men's
dining room."
sign at country club

"Wish – to end all the killing in the world. Hobbies –
hunting and fishing."
Bryan Harvey, baseball player

"Will the owner of a lost small black case containing a
hearing aid please identify himself by pressing the call
button."
*announcement from an airport public
address system*

"We'll be right straight back after this word from Doeskin Tissues: the very best Kleenex you can buy!"
Kate Smith, talk show host

"Reports are sketchy, but we have heard that in the first heart transplant operation in Belgium, both patient and donor are doing fine."
radio news announcement